CENGAGE Learning

Drama for Students, Volume 27

Project Editor: Sara Constantakis Rights Acquisition and Management: Mardell Glinski Schultz, Barb McNeil, Tracie Richardson, Robyn Young Composition: Evi Abou-El-Seoud Manufacturing: Drew Kalasky

Imaging: John Watkins

Product Design: Pamela A. E. Galbreath, Jennifer Wahi Content Conversion: Katrina Coach Product Manager: Meggin Condino

For product information and technology assistance, contact us at **Gale Customer Support, 1-800-877-4253.**

For permission to use material from this text or product, submit all requests online at **www.cengage.com/permissions.**

Further permissions questions can be emailed to **permissionrequest@cengage.com**
While every effort has been made to ensure the reliability of the information presented in this publication, Gale, a part of Cengage Learning, does not guarantee the accuracy of the data contained herein. Gale accepts no payment for listing; and inclusion in the publication of any organization, agency, institution, publication, service, or individual does not imply endorsement of the editors or publisher. Errors brought to the attention of the publisher and verified to the satisfaction of the publisher will be corrected in future editions.

Gale
27500 Drake Rd.
Farmington Hills, MI, 48331-3535

ISBN-13: 978-0-7876-8123-4
ISBN-10: 0-7876-8123-7
ISSN 1094-9232

This title is also available as an e-book.
ISBN-13: 978-1-4144-4939-5

ISBN-10: 1-4144-4939-9

Contact your Gale, a part of Cengage Learning sales representative for ordering information.

Printed in the United States of America
1 2 3 4 5 6 7 14 13 12 11 10

The Trojan Women

Euripides 415 BCE

Introduction

Euripides' *The Trojan Women* is acknowledged to be among the greatest surviving pieces of Greek tragedy. Although it won only second place in the City Dionysia, a dramatic festival, when it premiered in 415 BCE, it endured throughout antiquity in learned literary anthologies that helped to educate taste and reinforce Greek identity. Though it fell into disfavor during the Renaissance because of its flawed form, it has become one of the most commonly staged and adapted Greek dramas in the twentieth century because of its antiwar sentiment (often greatly exaggerated in modern productions and adaptations, such as that by Jean-Paul Sartre).

The Trojan Women tells the story of the women who survived the Greek capture of their city at the end of the Trojan War. They were destined to become the slaves of the victorious Greeks because the women's husbands, brothers, and fathers had all been slaughtered by their conquerors. Its very subject matter is subversive of the Greek heroic ideals expressed in Homer's *Iliad*, the great epic of the Trojan War. There are four main characters: Hecuba, who dominates the entire play, and her daughter and daughters-in-law, each of whom takes the lead in one act of the play. The first of these is the Trojan princess Cassandra, who is driven mad by the gods. Next is Andromache, who is forced to become the concubine to the Greek hero Neoptolemus, the son of Achilles, who had killed her husband Hector in battle. Third is Helen, who is condemned to death for adultery but is pardoned because of her beauty and, in Euripides' version, for her clever sophistic arguments. Finally, the Trojan queen Hecuba, present throughout the play, is left alone at the end to bury her infant grandson, whom the Greeks had murdered out of fear of the vengeance he might one day take if he grew to manhood. With its deep concern for injustice and impiety, *The Trojan Women* also reveals the stresses on Athens as it prepared to renew the Peloponnesian War at the end of the Peace of Nicias.

Author Biography

It is thought that Euripides was born in Athens in 480 BCE. Knowledge of his life is based on an anonymous biography that is sometimes attached to manuscripts of his plays and that was probably composed hundreds of years after his death. A few other sources of information are contained in even later Byzantine (medieval) encyclopedias. These sources are often contradictory, and there is little way of establishing an accurate version of his biography. Much of the material in these sources is actually reworked from Euripides' plays, as if they were autobiographical; other material is drawn from the comedic plays of Aristophanes, in which Euripides sometimes appears as a character. This situation is typical of many ancient authors. In the case of Euripides, all of the surviving material has been collected and translated into English by David Kovacs in *Euripdea*.

His family background is obscure, but he either was wealthy himself or could secure wealthy patrons to produce his plays. He began to compete in the annual Athenian dramatic festival of the City Dionysia in 456 BCE; he entered in twenty-two different years but won the first prize only four times (and once more posthumously). Posterity was kinder to him, however. All three of the surviving tragedians wrote about a hundred plays, but of Euripides' works, eighteen tragedies and one satyr play still exist, compared with seven tragedies each for Aeschylus and Sophocles. The tetralogy (a set of three dramas and a satyr play) of which *The Trojan Women* was a part premiered in 415 BCE and took second place. His other notable plays include *Medea* (431 BCE), *Electra* (420 BCE), and the posthumously produced *Bacchae* (405 BCE). Supposedly, Euripides became disenchanted with his popular and critical failure in Athens, and in 408 BCE he accepted an invitation to join the court of Archelaus, the king of Macedonia, in northern Greece. Euripides died in 406 BCE, about a year after he moved there. The sources provide various elaborate means of his death (for example, being poisoned by rival poets jealous of his talent), but since Euripides was by then seventy-four years old, his death requires no fantastic explanation.

Euripides explored to an unparalleled degree the ideas of science, philosophy, and rhetoric that dominated the intellectual life of fifth-century BCE Athens. For this reason, the sources make him a close associate of such famous philosophers as Anaxagoras, Protagoras, Prodicus, and even Socrates, but that list could just as well be a selection of figures approximately Euripides' age. In any case, Euripides' plays are certainly an exceptional component of the intellectual and cultural achievement of classical Athens.

Plot Summary

Greek tragedies were divided into episodes in which the actors sing and speak, advancing the plot, and *stasima* (choral odes) in which the chorus dances and sings, usually commenting on the development of the plot in the preceding episode.

Prologue, Lines 1-97

The play begins with a conversation between the gods Poseidon and Athene. Although no stage directions are given in the original manuscripts, it is probable that the gods were lowered onto the stage by cranes, symbolizing their heavenly nature. Poseidon is the first to appear. He names himself as the patron of Troy's people and laments that his city has been destroyed by Athene. He establishes the scene of the play as a hill overlooking Troy (also known as Ilium), which was probably visible in the background as scenery painting. He briefly describes the end of the siege, beginning with the deception of the Trojan Horse, and centering on the acts of impiety committed by the victorious Greeks (frequently called Achaeans) that have left the gods' temples empty and defiled. He starts with the murder of Priam, the king of Troy, who sought sanctuary at the altar of Zeus. According to Greek sacred law, Priam ought to have been safe as long as his hand was on the altar, but the Greeks broke that compact and killed him on the altar. More fundamentally, Poseidon points out that the destruction of Troy ends the very considerable worship that the gods received from Troy in the form of frequent sacrifices and the divine treasuries stored in the city's temples.

Poseidon explains that the war is over. The Greek ships are loaded with the sacred and public treasures of Troy, and the last thing to go on board will be the Trojan women, together with their children. Now enslaved, they are all that is left of the people of Troy since all adult men have been killed. The women are even now being assigned to individual Greek masters while they wait in an encampment of tents. Poseidon mentions by name Helen, the cause of the war, and Hecuba, the queen of Troy. He also mentions in particular two of the daughters of Hecuba and Priam: Polyxena, who has already been killed as a human sacrifice at the tomb of Achilles (the greatest Greek hero, who nevertheless died in battle a few months before the end of the war), and Cassandra, whom the god Apollo has driven mad. Poseidon laments that Troy has been destroyed because just as the Greeks overcame the Trojans, the will of Hera and especially that of the warrior goddess Athene overcame his own.

Athene appears and surprises Poseidon by asking him to help her punish the Greeks by sending storms to wreck their fleet on the homeward voyage across the Aegean Sea. She wishes to do this because the Greeks allowed the hero Ajax to pull Cassandra away from the temple of Athene, where she had sought sanctuary, thus committing sacrilege and insulting her. Naturally, Poseidon agrees.

Media Adaptations

- In 1824, the French poet Casimir Delavigne prepared a version of Euripides' *The Trojan Women* for singing as a cantata.

- In 1954, the French composer Paul Danblon composed an oratorio, *Les Troyennes*, based on Euripedes' drama, with a French libretto (lyrics) by Jean Le Paillot.

- In 1971, Michael Cacoyannis directed *The Trojan Women*, a film adaptation starring Katharine Hepburn, Vanessa Redgrave, Brian Blessed, and Patrick Magee. It was released on DVD by Kino Video in 2004.

- Elizabeth Swados composed a 1974 opera, *The Trojan Women*, loosely based on Euripides' original.

- The Greek composer Eleni Karaindrou composed incidental music for *The Trojan Women* in 2001.

Parodos, Lines 98-234

The chorus dances onto the stage through the doors in the *skene*, or backdrop to the action. The scene begins with Hecuba already on stage, that is, in the open air of the Trojan women's camp where she had slept during the night. It is now dawn. She sings a song lamenting that Helen ever came to Troy and her own consequent reversal of fortune (typical of tragic plots) from queen of Troy to slave groveling before the smoldering city. She tells the chorus, composed of the other captive Trojan women, that she cannot bear to see Cassandra, since she has been driven mad on top of all her other suffering. She also informs them that the Greeks have decided to take the women as spoils and leave Troy that very day, rather than slaughtering them as they had the men, a fate some of the women feared. The other women echo Hecuba's lament, hoping that they at least do not have to go to Sparta and serve the hated Helen. (Helen's husband, Menelaus, is the king of Sparta.)

First Episode, Lines 235-510

The Greek herald Talthybius now enters the stage, accompanied by some of the soldiers guarding the camp. He delivers the news that each of the Trojan women has been allotted individually as a slave to one of the Greeks. He reveals that Cassandra has been given to Agamemnon as his concubine. Hecuba laments that this as an act of impiety, since her daughter was devoted to lifelong virginity in the service of Apollo. Hecuba asks about her other daughter, Polyxena. Talthybius hints at the truth, but Hecuba perhaps does not wish to understand. She changes the subject to Andromache, who has been given to Achilles' son Neoptolemus. Hecuba herself has been allotted to Odysseus. This is the worst news for her yet, since she especially hates Odysseus as the deviser of Troy's defeat. She laments:

> To be given as slave to that vile, that
> slippery man,
> right's enemy, brute, murderous
> beast,
> that mouth of lies and treachery, that
> makes void
> faith in things promised.

The chorus leader (*coryphaeus*) asks what will become of all the other Trojan women, but no answer is ever given. Their fate is the anonymity of slavery.

Talthybius orders the guards to get Cassandra from her tent, taking her first because she is the property of Agamemnon, who rules over all the other Greeks. As they go to get her, however, she lights a torch inside her tent. This panics Talthybius because he fears the women plan to burn themselves to death rather than become slaves. He asks, "Have they set themselves aflame *in longing for death?" Before the guards can act, Cassandra dances out of the tent, performing the kind of hymn appropriate to a wedding and hence carrying a torch. Since she is by no means going to be properly married to Agamemnon, Hecuba and the others take this as a sign of her madness. However, Cassandra goes on singing and reveals that she is happier than any bride because she will be able to take revenge for her family and city by murdering Agamemnon, a perfectly rational and honorable wish in the ancient Greek context (other versions of this myth more often make Agamemnon's wife, Clytemnestra, the murderer of Agamemnon and Cassandra). She insists that although the Trojans died honorably fighting in defense of their city, the Greeks have actually suffered more since they lost thousands of soldiers merely to reclaim Helen, who willingly committed adultery, and Agamemnon himself had to sacrifice his own daughter, Iphigenia, before the gods would let the Greek armada set sail at the beginning of the war. This very clear threat and well-reasoned analysis of the Greek situation Talthybius dismisses as evidence of her madness, perhaps because admitting these truths would be unthinkable to him. Cassandra finally turns to prophecy and reveals that Apollo has told her Hecuba will die before leaving Troy and that Odysseus will be doomed to wander through ten more years of suffering before returning home. Hecuba ends the episode with a long lament for her reversal of fortune, finishing with the famous final line: "Of all who walk in bliss* call not one happy, until the man is dead."

First Choral Ode, Lines 511-576

As the chorus dances, its song recalls how happy the women had been when it had seemed the war was over, how they celebrated as the Trojan Horse (supposedly a gift) was brought into the city to be dedicated at the temple of Athene, but then how Odysseus and his Greeks crept out of the Horse and brought about the fall of the city and all its attendant disasters.

Second Episode, Lines 577-798

Andromache and her son, Astyanax, are brought on stage in a wagon containing the arms of her husband, Hector, and other spoils of war. She finally reveals to Hecuba that Polyxena was sacrificed at Achilles' tomb, as she herself witnessed. Andromache tells Hecuba that Polyxena is better off, for the dead experience nothing, while she herself must now betray her dead husband while at the same hating Neoptolemus, the man who will father more children on her. Hecuba advises Andromache that instead she ought love her new master and make him love her, for in that way it might someday become possible for Astyanax (who is the rightful king of Troy) or his son to return to Troy and rebuild the city. That is the only thing they can hope for, however unlikely. Talthybius returns and announces to the two women that he must tell them something so horrible it wishes he did not have the duty to speak it. The Greeks, persuaded by Odysseus, have decided to kill Astyanax by throwing him down from the walls of Troy. Only in this way can they be sure that he will not take revenge against them once he has grown up. When Talthybius moves to take the child, he urges Andromache not to resist and not to curse the Greeks, lest they go even further and leave the child unburied and without the religious rites for the dead.

Second Choral Ode, Lines 799-859

As the chorus again goes into its dance, its song recalls the myth in which Hercules and Telamon (father of Ajax and uncle of Achilles) sacked Troy in the time of Laomedon, Priam's father. They recall also that the gods once loved Troy; that Zeus took his cupbearer, Ganymede, from Troy; and that Eos, the goddess of the dawn, married the Trojan Tithonus, but now the gods have abandoned the city to destruction.

Third Episode, Lines 860-1059

Menelaus, the king of the Greek city of Sparta and legal husband of Helen, now comes to take his wife from the camp. He says that he has little interest in her, but he came to Troy to take revenge on Paris, who violated his hospitality in stealing her away, although that debt has long since been paid by Paris' death and now again by the destruction of Troy. He intends to take her back to Greece and execute her for the blood of all the Greeks spilled because of her adultery. As his soldiers bring Helen out of her tent, Hecuba urges Menelaus to instead execute her at once:

> Kill your wife, Menelaus, and I will
> bless your name.
> But keep your eyes away from her.
> Desire will win.
> She looks enchantment, and where she
> looks homes are set fire;
> she captures cities as she captures the
> eyes of men.

Told what her husband intends, Helen demurely asks permission to argue for her life. Menelaus agrees, and he also agrees to let Hecuba give a prosecution speech. The two women go over the facts of the case in the rhetorical language of the law courts, and Helen, in particular, argues in the manner of the sophists, actually echoing the arguments of the sophist Gorgias's demonstration speech in defense of Helen. The chorus responds to her with the charge typically leveled against sophists by more conservative elements of Greek society, that she is using the persuasive power of clever rhetoric to advance unjust and immoral arguments. Hecuba, however, persuades Menelaus that Helen indeed deserves to die for her crimes, and he leads her off to his ships in the expectation of having her stoned to death once they return to Greece.

Third Choral Ode, Lines 1060-1122

As the chorus dances, its members sing a lament that Zeus, in dooming Troy to destruction by the Greeks, has brought about the end of his own worship in the rich cults of the city, that they will never be able to bury their husbands and give their graves the religious service demanded by tradition, and finally that, while they themselves will be slaves in an alien land, they hope that the ship bearing Helen will be wrecked at sea and drown her before she can resume her life as queen of Sparta.

Exodos, Lines 1123-1322

The performance of the text becomes more musical, and eventually the chorus and actors dance off the stage, back through the skene. Talthybius returns, bearing the body of Astyanax. He gives it to Hecuba for burial, together with Hector's shield to serve as casket. She cleans and dresses the corpse and buries it, lamenting in song her sad fate and that of her family and nation. The only balm to her grief is the fact that her family will surely be remembered in song in later ages, a reference to the whole Homeric cycle of the Trojan War, but surely also to Euripides' own play. As he leads Hecuba and the other women away to their Greek masters, Talthybius gives the orders for the city of Troy to be set fire for its final destruction (this may have been shown as some kind of special effect on stage). Hecuba tries to throw herself into the flames but is restrained by her guards.

Characters

Tragedies were performed by three actors, who took all of the parts in turn. *The Trojan Women* is unusual in that the first actor (*protagonist*) played a single character, Hecuba, who is never off stage. The second actor (*deuteragonist*) probably played Poseidon, Cassandra, Andromache, and Helen, while the third actor (*tritagonist*) probably played Athene, Talthybius, and Menelaus.

Andromache

By virtue of being the widow of the Trojan prince Hector, Andromache is the daughter-in-law of Hecuba and mother of Astyanax. She is the main character of the second episode of the play. Euripides presents her as the epitome of the Greek conception of female virtue. She spent her days in the house engaged in domestic labor, such as weaving, and demurely submitted to her husband in all but household affairs. However tempted she was to learn of the world through education or experience, she sacrificed that desire to keep her good name, not even leaving the house to get water at a well. The Greek audience would understand that this kept her safe from the suspicion of adultery, the charge most shameful to Greek women and their husbands. Her purity was so great that it became known to the Greeks and caused her to be selected as concubine by Neoptolemus, the son of

Achilles, who killed Hector. The most hateful part of the prospect before her is that she now must betray her husband, to whom she wishes to remain loyal even after he has died. Hecuba advises her that she must ingratiate herself with her new master for the sake of her son. However, when the news comes that Astyanax is to be killed, she is left without even that hope.

Astyanax

Astyanax is the son of Andromache and grandson of Hecuba. He is the rightful king of Troy after the death of his father, Hector, and his grandfather, Priam. (His name means "king of the city.") He is murdered by the Greeks on the advice of Odysseus because "a hero's son could not be allowed to live" and someday take vengeance against any of those who destroyed his city and family. Astyanax is certainly no older than two years and is a nonspeaking role. Whether he was represented on stage by an actual child or by some sort of dummy is unknown.

Athene

Athene (also spelled Athena) is the goddess who stirred up the Trojan War out of rivalry with the goddess Aphrodite over which was the fairest. Originally, Athene had helped the Greeks to attack the Trojans, because Aphrodite had given Helen to the Trojan prince, Paris, in return for judging Aphrodite's beauty superior. However, by the beginning of *The Trojan Women*, the Greeks had offended Athene by desecrating her temple in Troy, and she plots with Poseidon to take revenge on them.

Cassandra

Cassandra is the last surviving daughter of Priam and Hecuba. She is the main character of the first episode of the play. Poets had considerable leeway in how to portray relatively minor characters like this. Euripides presents her as a priestess of Apollo who had been dedicated to perpetual virginity (an extremely rare situation in ancient religions), but "whom Agamemnon, in despite of the gods' will / and all religion, will lead by force to his bed." Apollo possessed her shortly before the beginning of the play. In Greek thought, possession did not entail a spirit entering the victim's body. Instead, the god merely touched her and she was driven mad. Other treatments of Cassandra have her give true prophecies of the future that are not believed. She does this too in *The Trojan Women*, with respect to Odysseus's wanderings. However, Euripides also gives her a similar role when she presents her concise analysis of the Greek situation, pointing out that they suffered more in their victory than the Trojans did in defeat. The Greeks reject this analysis as irrational, although it is all too plausible.

Hecuba

Hecuba was formerly the queen of Troy and is the mother of Polyxena and Cassandra, mother-in-law of Andromache (through her son Hector, killed during the war by the Greek hero Achilles), and grandmother of Andromache's son Astyanax. She is the main character of the play. As queen, she suffers the greatest reversal of fortune and the greatest suffering through the loss of her family and city and, especially, through the fates of her daughters and grandson. Hecuba is completely overwhelmed by the enormity of her loss and can attempt to discharge her grief only through hostility toward those she perceives as responsible for it, such as Odysseus and Helen.

Throughout the play, whenever Talthybius delivers some horrible news, Hecuba puts the best possible interpretation on it, so that through a dialectical discussion with the herald, the full extent of the new misfortune is only gradually revealed. This builds up tension and fear in the audience, who must wonder what will eventually be revealed. For instance, when Hecuba is told that her daughter Cassandra will become Agamemnon's slave, she first imagines that Cassandra will be a maid to the king's wife, Clytemnestra (itself a horrible fate because she is sister of the hated Helen), only to be told that she will become Agamemnon's concubine, an act of sacrilege and so an even greater outrage. She frequently feels herself so utterly powerless that there is nothing left for her to do but cry out, "Tear face, beat bosom," referring to stylized acts of public grieving in Greek culture.

In her debate with Helen, Hecuba is capable of making her own references to the philosophy of fifth-century BCE Athens. When she invokes Zeus, she follows the teachings of the philosopher Anaxagoras, suggesting that Zeus may be a physical principle or natural law, rather than an anthropomorphic (human-like) deity.

Helen

Helen, the most beautiful woman in the world, was offered to Paris by Aphrodite as a bribe for judging Aphrodite more beautiful than Athene and Hera, setting in motion the events that led to the Trojan War. Menelaus, her legitimate husband, recovers his wife after the war and determines to execute her for adultery. However, as the main character of the third episode of the play, she engages in a sort of legal process whereby she defends herself against the capital charge, and Hecuba acts as the prosecutor. Euripides uses the device to make Helen, the worst transgressor of proper social roles because of her adultery, a symbol of sophistry, which many Greeks felt was a more fundamental transgression of social norms of right and justice, because of its duplicitous use of rhetoric. Helen's speech is filled with the technical legal language created by the sophists: "Think what this means, and all the consequence…. You will all say this is nothing to the immediate charge…. I have witnesses."

After Helen is finished, the coryphaeus accuses

her in terms typical of the criticism directed at sophists: "She speaks / well, and has done wickedly. This is dangerous." But Helen and Hecuba both use the same technique that was the essential ingredient in ancient rhetorical discourse and especially in the teaching of the sophists: the appeal to plausibility. They both present facts, and even agree on many points of fact, but each insists that her own interpretation is the more plausible.

Helen begins by saying that Hecuba herself and Priam are the true cause of Troy's destruction because they had received clear prophecy that if they let their infant son Paris live, he would destroy the city, and yet they spared his life twice (this had been the subject of *Alexander*, the first play in Euripides' trilogy of 415 BCE, which the audience would have seen earlier in the morning of the day they saw *The Trojan Women*). She reminds Menelaus that if Paris had picked either Hera or Athene in the goddesses' contest, Paris might not have kidnapped her, but the gods would have given the Trojans the power to conquer Greece, so he was actually injured less by her adultery than if she had remained faithful. Next, Euripides has Helen echo the arguments put forth in the play *Helen* of the sophist Gorgias, the defense speech he had publicly delivered to demonstrate his rhetorical skill for arguing in favor of so obviously an indefensible case. Like Gorgias, she claims she was compelled to leave with Paris by force, that she was powerless to resist the gods who wished her to go.

Hecuba replies to Helen that the talk of

goddesses being subject to vanity is so much nonsense, as is Aphrodite aiding Paris in his abduction of her. The only 'Aphrodite' (who represents love) involved had been Helen's own desire. That is what persuaded her to betray her husband. Moreover, she had preferred to be a princess in Troy, a state far richer than the cities controlled by Menelaus. Hecuba bears witness that once the siege began, Helen had tormented Paris with jealously by threatening to slip over the wall and return to Menelaus. Indeed, Hecuba herself had offered to help Helen leave, but she did not. She certainly made no effort to kill herself, which is what Greek morality demanded of a woman in her position. Hecuba persuades Menelaus, who, acting as judge, condemns her to be publicly stoned to death, but back in Greece. The audience, however, knows, from the *Odyssey* (and the chorus suspects) that Helen will still be alive ten years later, with Menelaus once more submissively in love with her beauty.

Menelaus

Menelaus is the husband of Helen, whose adultery led to the Trojan War. Once he recovers her after the war from among the other Trojan women, he condemns her to death for her betrayal. Although he remains resolved on this throughout the play, other mythic sources, such as the *Odyssey*, suggest that Hecuba is correct in thinking he will eventually relent, being again captivated by her beauty.

Poseidon

Poseidon, god of the sea, begins the play with a prologue that describes the Greek capture of Troy. He laments the acts of sacrilege committed by the Greeks and the consequent failure of worship the gods will receive from Troy. When Athene proposes that they should join together to punish Greek impiety, he is highly suspicious of her because until that moment she had been on the Greek side, but nevertheless he eagerly joins in her plan.

Talthybius

Talthybius is the Greeks' herald, charged with communicating their decisions to the Trojan women. He was evidently chosen for this task because he had been known at the Trojan court before the war. He frequently laments that he has no taste for delivering the cruel and horrible news that he must tell Hecuba time after time, suggesting that even an ordinary Greek can be disgusted by the excesses they are forced to commit by war.

Catharsis

The earliest critics of Greek tragedy were two philosophers who lived in the generation after its peak, Plato and Aristotle. Both agreed that the function of tragedy was to arouse intense emotions. Plato feared that this process would tend to degrade the emotional life of the audience members and cause them to become worse people. He regretted that he could find little alternative to giving up tragedy. Aristotle, in the *Poetics*, was more pragmatic and viewed tragedy in a very different light.

Topics for Further Study

- Read through the Greek myths

retold for young audiences in *D'Aulaires' Book of Greek Myths*. Select one of them and write a brief dramatic scene based on part of it. Perform the scene for your class, with some of your classmates reading the various parts.

- Euripides most likely had in mind the wars his city was involved in when he wrote *The Trojan Women*. Find an interesting news story about events in Iraq or Afghanistan. Write an interpretation of the event, or a reaction to it, in the form of a brief dramatic scene.

- Helen is the most scandalous figure in Greek mythology. Research, write, and read for your class a defense or prosecution speech for a famous figure from American history, such as Marilyn Monroe (a sex symbol whose popularity did not stop her falling into depression and suicide) or Victoria Woodhull (a leading Spiritualist medium and the first woman to run for U.S. president in 1876). Do not limit yourself to a legal context, but consider how the life of the chosen figure conflicted with morality of her period.

- Herodotus and Thucydides, historians contemporary with

Euripides, began their works with extensive treatments of the Trojan War and of Helen in particular. How do their presentations of Helen differ or agree? How do they compare with Euripides' in *The Trojan Women*? Research these questions and present your findings to your class in the form of a PowerPoint presentation.

Aristotle believed that tragedy derived its emotional power from the imitation of events in real life, particularly because it did not show the audience the most pleasant aspects of existence but rather forced them to consider the most unpleasant aspects. Paradoxically, "though the objects themselves may be painful to see, we delight to view the most realistic representations of them in art." Tragedy achieved this goal through showing "incidents arousing pity and fear, wherewith to accomplish its catharsis of such emotions." Catharsis means "cleansing," and it was the Greek word for the then common method of treating illness by forcing the patient to vomit. Aristotle means that the drama serves to heighten these emotions and thereby discharge them, so that the viewer experiences a pleasurable release of tension. Few dramas present a greater object of pity than Hecuba in *The Trojan Women*; she sees all of her sons killed in battle, witnesses the murder of her husband as he seeks sanctuary at a divine altar, and falls from the status of a queen to that of a slave.

The audience naturally shares her fear when each new announcement in the course of the play brings news that one of her daughters has been raped, murdered, or sent off into slavery, and finally watches her bury the corpse of her last remaining grandson with her own hands.

Injustice

In the oldest dramatic productions in the early fifth century BCE, it was customary for all three plays to deal with the same event in a more extended fashion. The only trilogy of this type that survives is Aeschylus' *Oresteia*, which concerns Agamemnon's son Orestes having to take revenge on his own mother, who had murdered his father. By the late fifth century BCE, it was more typical to have the three plays deal with different mythical episodes, but in 415 Euripides produced a trilogy that better corresponded to the older type. The three plays all treat material that comes from the mythical cycle of the Trojan War. Although they are not bound in the sense of telling parts of the same story, they all concern acts of injustice. The first is *Alexander*, which concerns the efforts of the brothers of the Trojan prince Paris (who was also called Alexander) to prevent him receiving his rightful inheritance and status. The second is *Palamedes*; it is the story of a Greek hero on whom Odysseus takes personal revenge by framing him for plotting to betray the Greeks to the Trojans, resulting in him being unjustly stoned to death. The third (and the only one whose text survives) is *The*

Trojan Women, which concerns many acts of moral injustice inherent in the legal enslavement of the women, but in particular it is about the unjust murder of the child Astyanax to prevent him trying to take revenge on the Greek heroes when he grows up. The plot of the accompanying satyr play, *Sisyphus*, is unknown, but its main surviving fragment is a logical exposition of atheism.

Persuasive Literature

Sophists (the name means "wise men" or "sophisticated men"), such as Gorgias and Protagoras, were teachers of rhetoric, or the art of public speaking, in fifth-century BCE Greece. They especially congregated in Athens, where the democracy fostered their activities. Before the existence of print or any other kind of mass media, when citizens would have to defend themselves or undertake prosecutions in court without the aid of a lawyer, and where a speech well delivered in the council could persuade other citizens to accept or reject an idea and shape the course of state policy, the ability to persuade through words that sophists taught was of paramount importance. However, as the sophists analyzed what kinds of appeals could persuade people, they came to the opinion that all beliefs and moral standards were relative, changing from city to city and time to time, and therefore, such institutions as religion and law or concepts of right and wrong were social conventions created by people. They concluded not that these could be ignored, but that they could be exploited; an audience's beliefs could be used to make audience members come to the conclusion desired by a skilled speaker. For these reasons, as much as they were highly sought out as teachers, they were hated by philosophers and intellectuals, especially the writers of tragedy and comedy, as well as the general public. To their critics, the sophists seemed to make the worse argument the better: that is, they made the less persuasive argument seem more persuasive and the morally inferior argument seem superior, or at least expedient. Sophists were sometimes prosecuted for impiety or atheism (which were crimes in ancient Athens, where the state and religion were indistinguishable). In traditional Greek thought, impiety arose from the inability to tell right from wrong and so would naturally be associated with sophistic rhetoric. Anaxagoras, for instance, was prosecuted for attempting to explain astronomy in mechanistic rather than mythological terms, and one of the chief factors in the conviction of the philosopher Socrates was his association in the popular mind with the sophistic movement. The sophist Gorgias delivered a public speech in praise of Helen of Troy, claiming that she was completely free of guilt, a shocking supposition in an Athenian society nearly paranoid about adultery, where the honor of men depended on their ability to control the behavior of the female members of their families. In *The Trojan Women*, Euripides engages many sophistic themes about the nature of justice and religion, and his character Helen gives a speech defending herself. Euripides also engaged the sophists on much more serious matters. In his lost *Sisyphus*, the satyr play produced in 415 BCE together with *The Trojan Women*, Euripides has the title character speak the most extreme statement of atheism in Greek literature:

> Then, when the laws were preventing men from doing violence openly, but they did it in secret, that was the moment I think when … some shrewdly intelligent and clever man invented for mankind fear of gods, so that there might be something to frighten bad men even if they do or say or think something in secret. From that time therefore he introduced belief in gods.

The satirical point of the play perhaps came when Sisyphus (famously condemned for attempting to deceive the gods by forever having to push an enormous boulder up a hill in the underworld, only to have it roll back down when he reaches the top) discovers the reality of divine punishment. Sophistic themes of atheism and impiety are hotly contested in a more serious vein in *The Trojan Women* itself, for example, during the debate between Hecuba and Helen.

Style

Greek Drama

Religious festivals in which actors represent characters in mythological scenes have been part of many cultures, but drama as it is known in the modern West began in Classical Athens, a period often considered a cultural high point in art, literature, and philosophy. Tragedy started out as part of the festival of the City Dionysia (celebrated in worship of the god Dionysus) in which a chorus of men would dance while singing a hymn. The choruses competed against each other for the honor of a prize. The word *tragedy* is formed from the Greek words for "goat" and "song," perhaps suggesting that the victorious *coryphaeus*, or leader of a chorus, was awarded a goat. By the late sixth and early fifth centuries BCE, these performances had become extended so that lengthy scenes from myth were enacted in great detail by the chorus in conjunction with up to three actors, who performed additional dialogue that made complete stories. There were three types of drama: tragedy, which dealt with mythological themes in a serious manner; satyr plays, which gave burlesque versions of myth (hence the modern word satire); and fantastic and surreal comedies.

The City Dionysia was held each year in late March or early April. The main part of the celebration was the presentation of a series of dramatic cycles over three days. Each of the tragedies retold a familiar Greek myth in the form of a play. On the first day, there was a parade in honor of the god to the theater of Dionysus at the foot of the Acropolis (a hill), ending with the performance of dances by each of the three competing choruses (who would later also appear in the dramas). Next came the sacrifice of bulls to Dionysus in the theater. Over the following three days, each of the competing dramatists presented a trilogy of three tragedies and one satyr play, to make up a tetralogy. Each dramatist not only wrote the plays but paid for the production from his own resources (or from those of a patron), meaning that only aristocrats could compete. The audience consisted of about 20,000 adult male Athenian citizens. Women were not generally permitted in the theater. The performances began in the morning and lasted all day. Three audience members were chosen at random to act as judges. On the final day of the festival, five comedies would be presented, each by a different comedian. Aristophanes was the most prominent comedian.

Tragedy

The most important tragedians (and the only ones with plays that still exist in their complete form) were Aeschylus, Sophocles, and Euripides. In later periods, their work was constantly edited and republished so much that they became part of the core identity of the entire Greek and Roman world, in the same way that Shakespeare is essential to the identity of English-speaking cultures. Dramas would receive only a single official performance, but popular plays from the past would often be performed after the annual competition was completed.

The plays alternated dialogue among the actors with choral odes in which the entire chorus (about fifty dancers) would come out and sing and dance in the *orchestra*, or circular dancing floor nearest the audience. A backdrop was provided by the skene, an architectural screen that could also contain painted scenery. The plays were necessarily set in one location and in real time (there were no changes of scenery or breaks between acts), as if the audience were witnessing an event as it unfolded. However, actors might go into the skene, particularly if they had to carry out some gruesome act such as murder, which was not allowed to be shown on stage. The actors and chorus could exit and enter the stage through the skene or from the wings on either side. In some cases, characters could enter from the wings on a cart (*ekkyklema*), either to represent a chariot or other wheeled vehicle, or because they were dead or dying. When gods appeared in a play, they would be lowered from the top of the skene by a crane (the famous *deus ex machina* literally "god from a machine"). The actors wore masks fixed in the predominant emotion of the characters they portrayed (though the masks might be changed while the character was offstage). The masks contained megaphones that would amplify their voices to the audience. The actors wore buskins (boots) or stilts more than a foot tall and their costumes consisted of long flowing robes that trailed on the ground. Three actors performed all the roles (and therefore played more than one part), and all actors were male, even if they portrayed female characters. While not fully sung, the actors' lines were probably not spoken, but chanted in some way, though little is known about this. Medieval plain chant might suggest something of the way the dialogue was performed, although some of the longer speeches, such as Cassandra's in *The Trojan Women*, were clearly sung in a more complex manner. There is almost no surviving record of what the music in tragedy was like. The music, however, was also composed by the playwright. The subject matter of tragedy was drawn mostly from the Homeric epics or from other legends concerning the kings of Greece in the mythical period around the Bronze Age.

In the aftermath of the defeat of Athens in the Peloponnesian War, the best writers, such as Menander, shifted to new comedy realistically depicting everyday life, and the art of tragedy declined. Revivals became more important than new work. Dramas composed in the Roman Empire, such as those by Seneca, were mostly intended to be read rather than performed. This kind of work was more directly influential on Renaissance dramatists such as Shakespeare and the French playwright Racine. However, once Greek drama was rediscovered in the Renaissance, the performance of these works became immensely popular and led to the birth of opera as an art form. Although the music of Greek plays was not as extensive or complex as that of opera, the essential unity of tragedy and opera was defended as late as the era of the opera composer Richard Wagner and the philosopher Friedrich Nietzsche in the nineteenth century, especially in the latter's book *The Birth of Tragedy*.

Historical Context

Trojan War

The Trojan War and the return of its Greek heroes from Troy is the subject matter of the Homeric poems the *Iliad* and the *Odyssey*. These are the final records of an oral tradition of poetry that had flourished in Greece for centuries before the introduction of writing. In the generations after their publication, many other works were composed, the so-called Epic Cycle, which filled in details of the war left out of the two great poems. These probably also reflected traditional material. Aristotle mentions in the *Poetics* that *The Trojan Women*, like many tragedies, expands material that is mentioned in one of these works, the now lost *Little Iliad*, which told the story of the Trojan Horse and the capture of the city.

The Trojan War began when a golden apple inscribed "To the fairest" was cast into the divine court on Mount Olympus by the goddess Eris (who represents strife). Three goddesses—Hera, Athene, and Aphrodite—disagreed over which one should receive it. They selected the Trojan prince Paris (also known as Alexander) to decide the issue. Each bribed him—Hera with the rule over the whole world and Athene with invincibility in battle—but Paris preferred Aphrodite's bribe, to take Helen, the most beautiful woman in the world, as his wife.

Helen, however, was already married to Menelaus, the king of Sparta, so Paris visited Menelaus as a guest and kidnapped Helen, taking her back to Troy. Before Helen's original marriage, her hand had been sought by every prince in Greece. Odysseus decided the issue in favor of Menelaus by trickery, in exchange for being given Helen's sister Penelope as his own bride. Each one of Helen's suitors had sworn to guarantee the marriage with military force if necessary, so Menelaus and his brother Agamemnon (king of the chief Greek city of Mycenae) led an army composed of contingents of all the Greek states to Troy. After a siege that lasted ten years, Odysseus devised a ruse whereby the Greeks pretended they were admitting the futility of the war and sailing away, but left behind a large wooden statue of a horse as an offering. The Trojans took this inside their city to dedicate it in Athene's temple. That night, while the people of Troy were distracted by celebrating their deliverance from war, Odysseus and a squad of men who were hidden in the horse crept forth to open the city gates and admit the Greek army, which had returned. After Troy fell to the Greeks in this way, the stage was set for Euripides' *The Trojan Women*.

Compare & Contrast

- **Bronze Age:** The Greek society presented by Homer is monarchic, ruled by kings whose authority depends on their family lineages.

Fifth Century BCE: Athens governs itself by the most radical democracy that has ever held power, in which every aspect of state policy is determined by a majority vote of qualified voters, and most officials are chosen randomly.

Today: Both the United States and Greece are examples of modern democracy. The United States is a representative democracy (also known as a republic) in which most decisions are made by elected officials without direct consultation of the popular will. Greece is a parliamentary democracy.

- **Bronze Age:** The complete destruction of cities by war (including the mass murder of civilians) is common; the archaeological record of the end of the Bronze Age is marked by a layer of destruction in almost every city in Greece, as well as Troy.

  Fifth Century BCE: The destruction of cities (including the murder and enslavement of the civilian population) remains common, as marked by the Athenian destruction of Melos.

  Today: The mass slaughter of

civilians is recognized as genocide, and while still all too common, is outlawed as a war crime.

- **Bronze Age:** The characters in literature set during the Bronze Ages by Homer or Euripides live in close contact with the divine world.

  Fifth Century BCE: Religion is inextricably bound up with social and political life and is a main public concern of citizens and the state, even though some intellectuals question the logical and metaphysical foundations of religion.

  Today: Religion is a matter of personal, private conscience, and the political and social realms are largely or entirely secular, a division never imagined in antiquity.

Peloponnesian War

The Peloponnesian War was a conflict between Greek city-states that grew from rivalry between the two leading cities, Sparta and Athens. The principal source of information about the war is the contemporary Athenian historian Thucydides.

After the defeat of the Persian attempt to conquer Greece in 480-479 BCE, Sparta, because of its superior infantry force, was the most powerful Greek state. However, Athens possessed the most powerful navy and was in control of the Delian League, an alliance of Greek city-states devoted to liberating Greek cities still occupied by Persia in Ionia (the Aegean coast of modern Turkey). As this goal was accomplished, Athens increasingly became an imperial power controlling its allies, and it was growing far more powerful than any other Greek state. Sparta protected its preeminent position by organizing the Peloponnesian League (named after the southern peninsula of Greece). The inevitable war between the two alliances lasted from 431 to 404 BCE. The first part of the conflict is generally known as the Archidamian War; in it, Sparta annually invaded Attica, ravaging the countryside around Athens and forcing the population to take shelter within the city walls of Athens, which the relatively primitive military technology of the Spartans could not attack. Athens was provided with food by sea. However, in 430 BCE, a serious plague broke out, killing more than thirty thousand Athenian citizens, including the leading politician Pericles. Athens maintained its naval supremacy, so both sides were essentially unable to attack the other. Military operations were also carried out elsewhere in Greece, and eventually, in the battle of Spachteria in 425 BCE, a group of about 300 Spartan soldiers were captured by the Athenians, a revolutionary event, since no Spartan had ever surrendered before. The Athenians threatened to execute these soldiers if the Spartans invaded Attica again. By 421 BCE, a truce between the two alliances, supposed to last for fifty years, was negotiated by the Athenian general Nicias.

Athens took advantage of the Peace of Nicias to strengthen itself by gaining new territory not allied with Sparta and therefore unaffected by the truce. In 416 BCE, Athens conquered and annexed the Aegean island of Melos. However, in 415 BCE, the year Euripides' *The Trojan Women* premiered, Athens undertook to conquer the island of Sicily in the western Mediterranean. However, the Sicilian expedition, led by the generals Nicias and Alcibiades, ended in disaster and the complete loss of the Athenian forces in Sicily. During the campaign, Alcibiades was prosecuted for impiety and defected to the Spartan side. On his advice, the Spartans seized and fortified the Attic village of Deceleia in 413 BCE, disrupting Attica as thoroughly as they had with their previous campaigns but at a fraction of the effort. This began the second phase of the war, known as the Decelean War. Surprisingly, Athens recovered from the Sicilian disaster, but it suffered civil war between democratic and oligarchic factions. Sparta began to receive money for the war from the Persian Empire, which it used to construct its own fleet. In 405 BCE, the Spartan commander Lysander caught the main Athenian battle fleet hauled up onto the beach at Aegospotami (on the Chersoneses straits, between Europe and Asia) and destroyed it. After this, the Athenians had no choice but to give their unconditional surrender, ending the war and Athens's position as a great power in 404 BCE.

Critical Overview

The first criticism of Euripides' *The Trojan Women* was delivered in 415 BCE by the judges of the City Dionysia; they awarded it only second place, behind the plays of the now largely unknown dramatist Xenocles. A generation later, Aristotle in the *Poetics* gives hints that Euripides suffered from the disconnection between popular and sophisticated taste. Aristotle reports that Euripides' rival playwright Sophocles "said that he drew men as they ought to be, and Euripides as they are," implying that audiences do not like to see men as they are. Aristotle adds his own comment that the popular criticism of Euripides for also dwelling on the reversal of fortune was mistaken. Aristotle had realized that suffering was paradoxically the key to the beauty of tragedy, and in no other tragedy is the heroines' suffering so intense and sustained.

Gilbert Murray, the great classicist and translator of the first half of the twentieth century, suggests in *Euripides and His Age* that "Euripides must have been brooding on the crime of Melos during the autumn and winter" of 416 BCE; Murray thus argues for the first time a link between the Athenian defeat of Melos and Euripides' play of 415 BCE. In the introduction to his translation *Greek Tragedies*, Richmond Lattimore is one of the staunchest defenders of the Melos connection, but he cautions that although it may have inflamed patriotic feeling at the time, *The Trojan Women* was directed not against Athenian imperialism so much as against war in general. However, even this supposition has been questioned, since Greeks of the fifth century BCE did not think of permanent peace as an attainable or even desirable condition. Therefore, more recent critics, such as Casey Dué in *The Captive Woman's Lament in Greek Tragedy*, tend to think of *The Trojan Women* as similar to Aristophanes' peace comedies as arguing for an end to a particular war, namely the Peloponnesian War, which, although it had brought Athens considerable strategic advantage, had also left the Attic countryside ravaged and a large proportion of the Athenian population reduced to refugee status, sheltering inside the city walls. Barbara Goff suggests that the connection to contemporary events is far from implausible but that it would have been made, or not made, by each individual audience member in 415 BCE.

Murray also deals with the other main theme of modern criticism, the play's form. He observes that the structure of *The Trojan Women* is unlike any other drama and is subversive of any ordinary Greek use of myth:

> But it tells the old legend in a peculiar way. Slowly, reflectively, with little stir of the blood, we are made to look at the great glory until we see not glory at all but shame and blindness and a world swallowed up in night.

Later critics point out many ways in which *The

Trojan Women violates the tenets of tragedy. For instance, although there is a reversal of fortune in Hecuba and other noble Trojan women becoming slaves, there is no moment of self-discovery in which a hero, such as Oedipus or Agamemnon in other plays, who thought himself happy realizes that his true condition is pitiable and wretched, as Judith Mossman points out in her article in *A Companion to Greek Tragedy*. It has often been observed that, as Goff puts it, the play is liable to "charges of excessive emotionalism, and lack of movement and development." Whatever the character of its antiwar message and whatever its formal defects, *The Trojan Women* was mostly ignored before the twentieth century and Murray's championing of it. In the last century, though, it has generally been acknowledged as among the best of the tragedies; it is among the most performed and the most frequently adapted, always to give it a more straightforward antiwar message.

What Do I Read Next?

- *D'Aulaires' Book of Greek Myths*, by Ingri and Edgar D'Aulaire, first published in 1961 and frequently reprinted since, gives short versions of the Greek myths as an introduction for younger readers unfamiliar with the material.

- The Nigerian playwright Femi Osofisan composed a play, *Women of Owu*, based on Euripides' *The Trojan Women*. It was first performed in 2004 and published in 2006. The setting is early modern Nigeria, but the play rather transparently criticizes the Second Gulf War.

- The foundational 1983 collection of essays, *Images of Women in Antiquity*, edited by Averil Cameron and Amélie Kuhrt, presents a range of studies about the lives of women in antiquity, covering settings from ancient Mesopotamia to medieval Celtic society but firmly anchored in the Greco-Roman world.

- In a 2006 book intended for a general audience, *The Trojan War: A New History*, Barry Strauss surveys the representation of the war in the *Iliad* that serves as the background to *The Trojan Women* in conjunction with the archaeological record of the Greek Bronze Age, which sometimes tells a story quite different from Homer's.

- In his 1997 study *The Fall of Troy in Early Greek Poetry and Art*, Michael J. Anderson demonstrates the importance of the fall of Troy not only in Greek literature but, for the first time, in Greek vase painting.

- Henry Treece's 1967 novel for young adults, *The Windswept City*, is set during the last days of the Trojan War.

- The French existentialist philosopher Jean-Paul Sartre wrote a play also called *Trojan Women* in 1965 that was translated into English in 1976. It is more of a comment on Euripides than a translation, and its message is decidedly against the postcolonial wars then raging around the globe, particularly the French conflict in Algeria.

Sources

Aristotle, *Poetics*, in *The Complete Works of Aristotle: The Revised Oxford Translation*, Vol. 2, Bollingen Series LXXI, edited by Jonathan Barnes, Princeton University Press, 1995, pp. 2315-20.

Dué, Casey, *The Captive Woman's Lament in Greek Tragedy*, University of Texas Press, 2006.

Euripides, *Fragments*, Vols. VII-VIII, Loeb Classical Library, translated by Christopher Collard and Martin Cropp, Harvard University Press, 2008.

―――, *The Trojan Women*, translated by Richmond Lattimore, in *Greek Tragedies*, Vol. 2, edited by David Greene and Richmond Lattimore, University of Chicago Press, 1958, pp. 247-95.

Furley, William D., *Andokides and the Herms: A Study of Crisis in Fifth-Century Athenian Religion*, Bulletin of the Institute of Classical Studies Supplement 65, University of London, 1996.

Goff, Barbara, *Euripides: Trojan Women, Duckworth Companions to Greek and Roman Tragedy*, Duckworth, 2009.

Goldhill, Simon, "The Language of Tragedy: Rhetoric and Communication," in *The Cambridge Companion to Greek Tragedy*, edited by P. E. Easterling, Cambridge University Press, 1997, pp. 127-50.

Gorgias, "Encomium of Helen," in *The Norton*

Anthology of Theory and Criticism, edited by Vincent B. Leitch, W. W. Norton, 2001, pp. 30-33.

Green, Peter, *Armada from Athens*, Doubleday, 1970.

Grene, David, and Richmond Lattimore, eds., Introduction to *Greek Tragedies*, University of Chicago Press, 1960.

Guthrie, W. K. C., *The Sophists*, Cambridge University Press, 1971.

Kagan, Donald, *The Peloponnesian War*, Viking, 2003.

Kovacs, David, *Euripdea*, Mnemosyne Supplement No. 132, E. J. Brill, 1994.

Lefkowitz, Mary L., "'Impiety' and 'Atheism' in Euripides' Dramas," in *Classical Quarterly*, Vol. 39, 1989, pp. 70-82.

Mossman, Judith, "Women's Voices," in *A Companion to Greek Tragedy*, edited by Justina Gregory, Duckworth, 2005, pp. 352-65.

Murray, Gilbert, *Euripides and His Age*, Henry Holt, 1913, pp. 128-39.

Nietzsche, Friedrich, *The Birth of Tragedy*, translated by Douglas Smith, Oxford University Press, 2000.

Thucydides, *The Peloponnesian War*, translated by Richard Crawley, Modern Library, 1982.

Vickers, Brian, *Towards Greek Tragedy: Drama, Myth, Society*, Longman, 1973.

Yunis, Harvey, *A New Creed: Fundamental Religious Beliefs in the Athenian Polis and Euripidean Drama*, Hypomnemata, No. 91, Vandenhoeck & Ruprecht, 1988.

Further Reading

Bushnell, Rebecca, ed., *A Companion to Tragedy*, Blackwell, 2005.

> The essays in this volume deal with ancient tragedy, its renaissance, and its modern reception.

Croally, N. T., *Euripidean Polemic: "The Trojan Women" and the Function of Greek Tragedy*, Cambridge University Press, 1994.

> Croally focuses on *The Trojan Women* to argue that the purpose of tragedy in Athenian society was to question tradition through the Socratic method.

Euripides, *Trojan Women*, translated by Diskin Clay, Focus, 2005.

> This recent translation focuses on stage performance by inserting extensive stage directions suitable for a modern production.

McDonald, Marianne, *The Living Art of Greek Tragedy*, Indiana University Press, 2003.

> This is a survey of Greek drama with a special emphasis on modern productions and modern adaptations

rather than merely translations.

Seneca, Lucius Annaeus, *Trojan Women*, translated by Frederick Ahl, Cornell University Press, 1986.

> This is an English translation of the play by the Roman playwright, philosopher, and politician Seneca. His version takes a very different approach from that of Euripides.